CU00848113

Windows NT
Desktop Reference

Æleen Frisch

O'REILLY™

Cambridge   Köln   Paris   Sebastopol   Tokyo

Windows NT Desktop Reference

by Æleen Frisch

Copyright © 1998 O'Reilly & Associates, Inc. All rights reserved.
Printed in the United States of America.

Published by O'Reilly & Associates, Inc., 101 Morris Street,
Sebastopol, CA 95472.

Editor: Mike Loukides

Production Editor: Jane Ellin

Printing History:

      January 1998:   First Edition.

ISBN: 1-56592-437-1   [6/98]

Table of Contents

Windows NT Desktop Reference

Introduction

This desktop reference documents Windows NT command mode. It includes most available Windows NT commands (a few commands designed for backward compatibility with DOS are omitted), as well as the most useful commands from the Resource Kits (which must be purchased separately from the operating system). Resource Kit commands are marked with a dagger in their header line.

Commands are arranged alphabetically. Consult the topical list of commands to locate a desired command. Command options are grouped by function and ordered by importance. Occasionally, unimportant options are omitted.

The information in this booklet corresponds to Windows NT 4.0, but much of it applies to earlier versions as well.

Conventions

cmd

    Denotes a Windows NT command or option.

arg

    Denotes variable text (things you must fill in).

[…]

    Denotes optional parts of commands.

a | b

    Indicates that one of **a** or **b** should be selected.

†

    Denotes a Resource Kit command.

Entering Commands

- Commands are not case sensitive.

- Command options are not usually case sensitive, and case-insensitive options are given in uppercase. Options which must be entered in lowercase are given in that form.

- Command options are usually preceded by a forward slash: **/X**. In many cases, a minus sign may be substituted for the slash. A few Resource Kit commands require their options to be preceded by a minus sign.

- Option placement is not consistent across all commands. Consult a specific command's syntax summary for option placement.

- Distinct command arguments are separated by spaces, commas, or semicolons.

- A command may be continued onto a second (or subsequent) line by placing a caret (^) as the final character of the preceding line.

- The caret character is also used as the escape character, protecting the following character from being processed by the command interpreter.

- Multiple commands may be concatenated by an ampersand: *command1* **&** *command2*. The commands are executed in sequence.

- Commands may be conditionally executed based on the success or failure of a preceding command by joining them with **&&** or **||**:

    command1 **&&** *command2*
    Execute *command2* only if *command1* succeeds.

    command1 **||** *command2*
    Execute *command2* only when *command1* fails.

List of Commands by Topic

Help Commands

help	net helpmsg
command /?	ntbooks
net help	
command	

General Purpose Commands

cmd	more
date	path
doskey	sort
find	time
findstr	ver

General Administrative Commands

net computer	net time
net name	shutdown†
net send	

Working with Directories

cd	pushd
md	rd
popd	

Working with Files

attrib	dir	ntbackup	tree
cacls	expand	perms†	type
comp	fc	rdisk	verify
compact	move	ren	xcopy
convert	net file	replace	
copy	net share	scopy†	
del	net use	srvcheck†	

Working with Disks and Filesystems

chkdsk	label
diskcomp	showdisk†
diskcopy	vol
format	

Accessing the System Registry

regback†
regrest†
scanreg†

Networking-Related Commands

net session
net statistics
net view

TCP/IP-Specific Commands

arp
dnsstat†
finger
ftp
hostname
ipconfig
nbtstat

netstat
nslookup
ping
route
telnet
tracert

Managing Processes

at
diskperf
kill†
net print
pmon†
pulist†
pview†

pviewer†
rkill†
soon†
start
timethis†
tlist†

Managing Services

instsrv†
net config
net continue
net pause
madd

net start
net stop
netsvc†
sclist†

Administering Users and Groups

global†
local†
net accounts
net group

net localgroup
net user
showgrps†
usrstat†

I/O Redirection

< file
>   Take standard input from a file.

> file
1> file
>   Send standard output to a file.

2> file
>   Send standard error to a file.

>> file
1>> file
>   Append standard output to a file.

2>> file
>   Append standard error to a file.

command1 | command2
command1 0> command2
>   Form a pipe, linking the standard output of *command1* to the standard input of *command2*.

Help Commands

help *command*
>   Obtain help for a standard Windows NT command.

command **/?**
>   Obtain help for the specified command.

net help *command*
>   Obtain help for one of the **net** commands.

net helpmsg *nnnn*
>   Explain Windows NT message number *nnnn*.

ntbooks
>   Open CD-based Windows NT documentation.

NTCmds.Hlp
>   Help file for built-in Windows NT commands.

RKTools.Hlp†
>   Help file for Resource Kit commands (located in the NTResKit directory).

Alphabetical List of Commands

arp

Display and manipulate physical address to IP address translation.

> **arp** /A [*IP-address*] [/N *interface-address*]

Display current mappings (limited to the specified IP address or network interface if present).

> **arp** /S *IP-address physical-address* [*interface-address*]

Specify an address mapping (to the table for the specified network interface if present).

> **arp** /D *IP-address* [*interface-address*]

Delete an address mapping (from the table for the specified network interface if present).

at

List or schedule delayed and periodic tasks on the specified computer system (defaults to the local system).

> **at** [*host*]

Without any arguments, **at** lists the current contents of the Schedule service queue.

> **at** [*host*] *job-ID* /DELETE
>
> **at** [*host*] /DELETE [/YES]

Remove a pending job (first form) or all pending jobs (second form; /YES preconfirms the action).

> **at** [*host*] *time* [*options*] *command*

Schedule a job for one-time or periodic execution. *time* indicates the time of day when the command will run.

Options

/NEXT:*weekday* | *n*

Run the command on the next occurrence of the specified day of the week or n^{th} of the month.

/EVERY:*weekday-and-dates-list*

Run the command on a regular schedule, on each day of the week and date of the month specified in the comma-separated list.

/INTERACTIVE

Allow desktop input when the command executes.

---

attrib

attrib [*options*] [*files*]

Set DOS file attributes (or display current attributes if no options are specified). The file list defaults to all files in the current directory.

Options

+*x*, **−***xS*

Add or remove an attributSe, where *x* is one of the following code characters: **R** (read-only), **H** (hidden), **S** (system), or**A** (archive).

/S

Recurse subdirectories in the file list.

---

cacls

cacls *files* [*options*]

Display (if no options are specified) or modify access control lists (ACLs).

Options

/T

Propagate changes to subdirectories in the file list.

/E

Edit the existing ACL (the default is to replace it).

/G *users:perm*

/P *users:perm*

Grant or replace (respectively) permissions in the access control entries (ACEs) for the specified users. *perm* indicates the defined permission set, one of **R** (Read), **C** (Change),**F** (Full control), or **N** (None; **/P** only).

/R *users*

Remove the ACE for the specified users (requires **/E**).

/D *users*

Deny specified users all access to the files.

/C

Continue applying changes even if an error occurs.

---

cd

cd [/D] [*path*]

Display or set the current working directory. If *path* does not include a drive letter, the current drive is assumed. Use **/D** to change the current directory on the specified drive when it is different from the current drive (the default is to set it).

chdir is a synonym for **cd**.

---

chkdsk

chkdsk *x*: [*options*]

Check the filesystem on drive *x*.

Options

/F

Fix any errors encountered.

/L:*n*

Change log file size to *n* KB (NTFS filesystems only).

/R

Locate and recover bad sectors.

/V

Produce verbose output.

---

cmd

cmd [*options*] [**/C** | **/K** *command*]

Start a new Windows NT command interpreter. If *command* is specified, that command is executed. Enclose multiple commands in quotation marks.

Use the **exit** command to end a command interpreter session.

Options

/C, /K

Carry out the specified command, retaining or terminating the command interpreter afterwards (respectively).

/Q

Disable command echoing (see **echo OFF**).

/X, /Y

Enable/disable (respectively) command interpreter extensions. The default is set by the value of the HKEY_CURRENT_USER\Software\Microsoft\Command Processor\Enable Extensions registry key (enabled by default).

/A, /U

Format command output as ANSI (default) or Unicode, respectively.

---

comp

comp [*options*] *fileset1 fileset2*

Compare two sets of files (or individual files). If multiple files are specified, files of the same name are compared. Differences are reported only for files of identical size (use **fc** to compare files of different sizes).

Options

/A

Display the differences in ASCII form (the default is decimal).

/L

Display line numbers for differing lines.

/C

Perform a case-insensitive comparison.

/N=*n*

Compare only the first *n* lines of each file.

---

compact

compact [*options*] [*files*]

Compress or uncompress the specified files, setting directories' default settings, or display the compression status of the specified files. If omitted, the file list defaults to the current directory and its contents.

See also **expand**.

Options

/C, /U

Specify a compression or uncompression operation (respectively).

/S

Recurse subdirectories in the file list.

/F

Force compression even on already compressed files (which are skipped by default).

/I

Continue processing files even if an error occurs.

/Q

Request terse output.

/A
Display hidden and system files, which are omitted by
default (these files are processed, however).

convert

convert *x*: **/FS:NTFS**

Convert drive *x* to an NTFS filesystem. Add the **/V** option for
more verbose output.

copy

copy [*options*] *source destination*

Copy files to *destination*. If *destination* is a single file, all
source files are concatenated (the form *file1* + *file2* + ... may
also be used to specify file concatenation).

Options

/A, /B
Designates an ASCII or binary file, respectively (precedes
a filename).

/V
Verify the copied data after writing.

/N
Use 8.3 (DOS-style) filenames for the copied files.

/Z
Perform a restartable network file copy operation.

date

date [*date*]

Set the date to the specified date (prompted if omitted). The
/T option displays the date without modifying it.

del

del [*options*] *files*

Delete files. **erase** is a synonym for **del**.

Options

/S

Recurse subdirectories in the file list.

/Q

Suppress all confirmation prompts.

/P

Confirm every deletion operation.

/F

Force delete read-only files.

/A:*codes*

Select only files with the specified attributes (**H** for hidden, **S** for system, **R** for read-only, **A** for archive).

---

dir

dir [*options*] [*path*]

Display directory contents. *path* defaults to the current directory.

Options

Options may be set in the DIRCMD environment variable. They may be overridden by including the option on the command line preceded by a minus sign (e.g., **/-N**).

/B

Display filenames only, one per line (omit header line).

/W, /D

Wide directory listing: display several filenames per output line, ordering them by row or column, respectively.

/N

UNIX-style long directory listing (filenames appear on the right).

/L

Display all filenames in lowercase.

/X

Show 8.3 (DOS-style) filenames in addition to long filenames.

/S

Recurse subdirectories.

/O:*sort-order*

Specify ordering of displayed files, using these codes: **N** (by name),**E** (by extension), **S** (by size), **D** (by date and time), **G** (list directories first). Precede any code letter with a minus sign to reverse the usual sort order.

/T:*timecode*

Select which time is displayed and used for sorting: **C** (creation time),**A** (access time), **W** (modification time, which is the default).

/A:*codes*

Select only files with the specified attributes (**D** for directories, **H** for hidden, **S** for system, **R** for read-only, **A** for archive). A minus sign before a code letter indicates that files of that type are to be excluded.

/C, /–C

Include/omit commas from file sizes (the default is to include them).

/P

Pause after each screen of output.

---

diskcomp

diskcomp *x*: *y*:

Compare the diskettes in drive *x* and drive *y* (may be the same drive).

diskcopy

diskcopy *x*: *y*: [/V]

Copy floppy in drive *x* to drive *y* (may be the same diskette drive). /V says to verify the copied data.

diskperf

diskperf -Y | -YE | -N [*host*]

Enable/disable disk performance counters on the specified system (defaults to the local system). The listed options enable normal counters, enable enhanced counter for striped disk sets, and disable all counters, respectively. The command takes effect once the system is rebooted.

dnsstat†

dnsstat *host* | *IP-address* [/C]

Display DNS server statistics for the specified host. The /C option clears those counters that can be cleared.

doskey

doskey [*options*]

Recall previous commands or create macros (aliases).

Command History and Editing Options

/HISTORY

Display entire command history list.

/LISTSIZE=*n*

Set the size of the history list to *n*.

/INSERT, /OVERSTRIKE

Set the default editing mode for recalled commands to insert or overstrike (generally the default) mode.

Macro Options

macroname=command

> Define a macro. Within *command*, **$T** inserts a command separator, **$1** through **$9** denote command arguments one through nine, and **$*** denotes all command arguments.

/MACROS:ALL

> Display all defined macros.

/MACROFILE=*file*

> Install all macros stored in the specified file.

/EXENAME=*exefile*

> Specify an executable file to associate with the macros being defined.

/MACROS:*exefile*

> Display all defined macros associated with the specified executable file.

---

expand

> **expand** [**/R**] *source* [*destination*]

Expand compressed files. **/R** says to rename the expanded files.

---

fc

> **fc** [*options*] *fileset1* *fileset2*

Compare files or sets of files, displaying the differences between them. If multiple source files are specified, files of the same name in the second file set are compared.

Options

/B, /L, /U

> Compare the files as binary files, ASCII text files, or Unicode text files, respectively.

/C

> Perform a case-insensitive comparison.

/W

Compress all white space before comparing.

/T

Don't expand tabs to spaces.

/LB*n*

Specify the maximum number of consecutive mismatches.

/*n*

Specify the number of consecutive matching lines required after a mismatch before the files are again considered synchronized (the default is 2).

/A

Limit the display to just the first and final lines of each set of differences.

/N

Include line numbers in the display (valid for text files only).

---

find

find [*options*] *string* [*files*]

Search for a literal text string in the specified files or standard input (via a pipe) or text entered at its prompt, and display matching lines.

Options

/V

Display only non-matching lines.

/I

Perform a case-insensitive search (case-sensitive is the default).

/C

Display only a count of matching lines.

/N

Display the line number preceding each line.

findstr

> **findstr** [*options*] /C:*string* | /G:*file* | *strings* [*files*]

Search for one or more text strings or regular expressions in
the specified files or standard input (if no files are given),
and display matching lines. Enclose multiple search strings in
quotation marks.

Options

/R

Interpret search strings as regular expressions.

/L

Interpret search strings as literal text.

/C:*string*

Designate the specified string as a literal text string (useful
for strings with internal spaces).

/G:*file*

Read the search strings from the specified file. A slash for
file says to read the filename from the console.

/B, /E

Match search string only if at the beginning or end of a
line, respectively (don't include both).

/I

Perform a case-insensitive search.

/V

Display non-matching lines.

/X

Display only lines that match exactly.

/N, /O

Precede displayed lines with their line number or character offset (respectively).

/M

Display only the names of files containing a match.

/S

Recurse subdirectories in file list.

/F:*file*

Read the file list from the specified file. A slash for *file* says to read the file list from the console.

/P

Skip files containing non-printable characters.

finger

finger [*user*][@*host*]

Display information about the specified local or remote user (the remote host must provide a finger service). If no user-name is specified, information is returned about all logged-in users.

format

format *x*: [*options*]

Format the disk partition designated by drive letter *x* (or the diskette in drive *x*:).

Options

/FS:*type*

Specify the file system type (**NTFS** or **FAT**).

/V:*label*

Specify the volume label.

/A:*n*

Set filesystem's allocation unit size to *n* bytes (add the K suffix to designate kilobytes). Valid sizes are powers of 2 from 512 to 64K for NTFS filesystems and 8192 to 16K for FAT filesystems.

The default allocation unit size varies with the partition size: 4K for filesystems over 2GB, 2K for 1–2GB, 1K for 513MB–1GB, and 512 for 512MB or less.

/C
> Compress files on the new filesystem by default (NTFS filesystems with an allocation size of 4K or less only).

/Q
> Perform a quick format operation if possible.

/T:*tracks*, /N:*sectors*
> Specify tracks/side and sectors/track (respectively) for floppy disks.

---

ftp
> **ftp** *host* | *IP-address*

Initiate a file transfer session to a remote host (which must provide an ftp service).

---

global†
> **global** *group domain* | *host*

List the members of a global group.

---

hostname
> **hostname**

Display the hostname of the local system.

---

instsrv†
> **instsrv** *service-name command-path* [*options*]

Install a new service with the specified service name, running the executable indicated by *command-path*.

> **instsrv** *service-name* **remove**

Remove an installed service. Use **sclist** to determine the name of the desired service.

Options

/A *user*

Run the service as the specified user account.

/P *password*

Specify the password for the user account.

---

ipconfig

ipconfig [/ALL]

Display the IP configuration for the local system (**/ALL** requests more detail).

ipconfig RENEW | RELEASE [*adapter*]

Manipulate the DHCP lease, renewing or releasing the system's IP address (or the IP address corresponding to the specified network adapter).

---

kill†

kill [/F] *item*

Terminate one or more processes, where *item* is a process ID or a regular expression that matches complete task/command names or window titles. The **/F** option kills some processes that survive the normal termination signal.

---

label

label [*x*:] [*label*]

Assign the volume label for drive *x* (default to the current drive). If no *label* is specified, you will be prompted for it.

---

local†

local *group domain* | *host*

List the members of a local group.

---

md

> md *path*

Create the specified directory (and all missing intermediate subdirectories). **mkdir** is a synonym for **md**.

more

> more [*options*] [/E *files*]

Display output or file contents one screen at a time. By default, **more** displays the data on its standard input.

Options

The command also uses any options set in the MORE environment variable.

/E
> Enable command's extended features (resulting in a UNIX-style **more** command). In this mode, the command may be given a list of files to display.

/C
> Clear the screen before displaying the first page.

/S
> Combine (squeeze) multiple blank lines into one.

/T*n*
> Expand tabs to *n* spaces (by default, tabs are expanded to eight spaces).

/P
> Expand form feed characters.

+*n*
> Begin the display at line *n* of the input or first file.

move

> move *files destination*

Move files to a new directory location.

nbtstat

> **nbtstat** [*options*] [*n*]

Display statistics for NetBIOS over TCP/IP connections
(repeating the display every *n* seconds if specified).

Options

-a *host*, **-A** *IP-address*
> Specify the host of interest by name or IP address.

-c
> Display contents of the remote name cache.

-n
> Display local NetBIOS name definitions.

-r
> Display names resolved by WINS or broadcast.

-S, -s
> Display the sessions table, identifying remote systems by
> IP address or hostname (respectively).

-R
> Purge and reload the remote name cache.

---

net accounts

> **net accounts sync**

Force an update of the user accounts database.

> **net accounts** *options* [**/DOMAIN**]

Modify system or domain password policy settings.
/DOMAIN says to operate on the primary domain controller
rather than the local system (it is the default on Windows NT
server systems).

Options

/MINPWLEN: *n*
> Set the minimum password length to *n* characters (the
> default value is 0, and the allowed range is 0–14).

/MAXPWAGE:*n*

Set the maximum password lifetime to *n* days (the default is 42, and the allowed range is 1–49710). The keyword **UNLIMITED** may be specified for *n* to remove any limit.

/MINPWAGE:*n*

Set the minimum number of days between password changes (the default value is 0, and the allowed range is 0–49710).

/UNIQUEPW:*n*

Remember *n* previous passwords (the default value is 0, and the maximum value is 24).

---

net computer

> **net computer** *host* /ADD | /DELETE

Add or remove the specified computer from the domain database.

---

net config

> **net config** [SERVER | WORKSTATION]

Display service configuration information. Without an argument, displays services for which configuration data is available. The available keywords display the configuration of the server or workstation service, respectively.

---

net continue

> **net continue** *service*

Resume a previously paused service.

---

net file

> **net file** [*id* [/CLOSE]]

Without arguments, list all open shared files and their ID numbers. When an *id* is specified, information about that item is displayed, and the **/CLOSE** option closes the file.

---

net group

Display/modify a global group. For all command forms, /DOMAIN says to operate on the primary domain controller rather than the local system (it is the default on Windows NT server systems).

net group

List global group names in the current domain.

net group *name* [*users*] [/ADD] [/DOMAIN]

Add a group, or add users to an existing group.

net group *name* [*users*] /DELETE [/DOMAIN]

Delete a group, or remove users from a group.

net group *name* [/ADD] /COMMENT:*description* [/DOMAIN]

Specify a description for an existing or a new group.

net localgroup

Display or modify a local group. For all command forms, /DOMAIN says to operate on the primary domain controller rather than the local system (it is the default on Windows NT server systems).

net group

List local group names in the current domain.

net group *name* [*users*] [/ADD] [/DOMAIN]

Add a group, or add users to an existing group.

net group *name* [*users*] /DELETE [/DOMAIN]

Delete a group, or remove users from a group.

net group *name* [/ADD] /COMMENT:*description* [/DOMAIN]

Specify a description for an existing or a new group.

net name

net name [*name*] [/DELETE]

Without parameters, the command displays the current name set (message recipients targeted to this user account). If an argument is included, it adds the specified name to the current name set.

The **/DELETE** option removes the specified name from the name set.

net pause

net pause *service*

Pause a running service.

net print

net print *host**shared-printer*

List contents of the specified print queue.

net print [*host*] *job-number* [/HOLD | /RELEASE | /DELETE]

List/manage the specified print job, performing the operation indicated by any specified option.

net send

net send *who message*

Send a message to one or more users. *who* may be one of the following:

- A username.

- A message recipient defined with **net name**.

- A hostname (corresponds to any user logged into the specified computer).

- An asterisk for all users in the local domain.

- **/DOMAIN:** *name* for all users in the specified domain.

- **/USERS** for all users with connections to the local server.

---

net session

net session [*host*] [/DELETE]

Without arguments, display session information for all connections to the local system. If a host is specified, information about the session between the local system and that remote system is displayed.

The **/DELETE** option causes the specified session (if a host is specified) or all sessions to be terminated, closing all associated open local files.

---

net share

net share *share-name*[=*path*] [*options*]

Make a directory available to the network or revoke shared access (the =*path* form is used only when defining a new shared resource).

Without arguments, the command lists all current shared resources. If just a share name is specified (without options), information about that resource is displayed.

Options

/USERS: *n*
> Specify the maximum number of simultaneous users.

/UNLIMITED
> Allow unlimited users to simultaneously access the share.

/REMARK: "*text*"
> Specify a description or other comment for the share.

/DELETE
> Remove the specified shared resource. Either the share name, path, or printer device may be specified as the argument to the command.

---

net start

net start *service*

Start a Windows NT service.

net start *lpdsvc*

Start the incoming LPD support service.

netstat

netstat [*options*] [*n*]

Display TCP/IP statistics (repeating the output every *n* seconds if specified). By default, current active connections are listed.

Options

/A

Include server-side connections.

/E

Display Ethernet statistics.

/N

Show numeric IP addresses and port numbers.

/R

Display the routing table.

/S

Display per-protocol statistics (specify desired protocol with **/P**).

/P *protocol*

Specify network protocol of interest (**TCP**, **UDP**, or **IP**).

net statistics

net statistics [**SERVER** | **WORKSTATION**]

Display networking statistics (session-oriented). Without an argument, displays services for which statistics are available.

The available keywords request statistics for the server or workstation services, respectively.

---

net stop

> **net stop** *service*

Stop the specified service.

---

netsvc†

> **netsvc** *service* *host* /*cmd*

Manage services on a remote host. *cmd* is one of: **list**, **query**, **start**, **stop**, **pause**, and **continue**.

---

net time

> **net time** *from* [/**SET**]   /ЧЕS

Display the system time on a specified system. /**SET** says to synchronize the local time with it. *from* takes the form *hostname* or /**DOMAIN**:*name*.

---

net use

> **net use** [*device*:] [*host**share*] [*password* | *] [*options*]

Map a network resource to a local device, which can be a drive letter or a printer of the form **LPT***n*.

The host and share name argument is used only when defining new mappings. It may have a NetWare volume name appended if appropriate.

Any required password may be specified on the command line, or an asterisk may be substituted to request a password prompt.

Options

/PERSISTENT:YES | NO
Create a persistent mapping (automatically recreated at each login). The default is the setting used most recently. If this option is specified without any other arguments, it changes the current default.

/USER:[*domain*]*username*
Specify an alternate user account for accessing the resource.

/HOME
Map the specified drive letter to your home directory (no resource specification is needed).

/DELETE
Permanently remove the specified device mapping.

---

net user

> **net user** *username* [*passwd* | *] [/ADD [*options*] | /DELETE] [/DOMAIN]

Create or modify user accounts. As indicated, the username can optionally be followed by a password or by an asterisk to request a password prompt. Without any arguments, the command will list all user accounts in the local domain (or on the local workstation).

Options

/ADD, /DELETE
Add or delete the specified user account. The default is to modify an existing account.

/DOMAIN
Operate on the primary domain controller rather than the local system (it is the default on Windows NT server systems).

/ACTIVE:YES | NO
Enables or disables the account.

/FULLNAME: *text*

User's full name.

/EXPIRES: *date* | **NEVER**

Account expiration date (if any).

/HOMEDIR: *path*

Home directory location.

/PASSWORDCHG: YES | **NO**

Whether user can change her password.

/PASSWORDREQ: YES | **NO**

Whether a password is required for this account.

/PROFILEPATH: *path*

Path to the user profile for this account.

/SCRIPTPATH: *path*

Location of this user's login script.

/TIMES:ALL | *times*

Allowed login hours.

/WORKSTATIONS: *list*

Limit allowed login locations to these systems (maximum of 8).

/COMMENT: *string*, **/USERCOMMENT:** *string*

Decriptive comments for the account.

/COUNTRYCODE: *n*

Operating system country code (0 means the system default).

---

net view

net view [*target*]

Display the names of computers in a domain or network or the shared resources on a specified remote system. *target* can be one of the following:

host

The name of a remote system whose shared resources are to be displayed.

/DOMAIN:*name*
> A Windows NT domain (its members are listed).

/NETWORK:NW [*host*]
> Without a hostname, this option lists all available NetWare servers. If *host* is included, the NetWare resources for the specified system are listed.

If no *target* is specified, then the computers in the local domain are listed.

---

nslookup

> **nslookup** [*name*]

Perform DNS name translation.

---

ntbackup

> **ntbackup** *op path* [*options*]

Perform a backup operation to tape, where *op* is either **backup** or **eject**.

Options

/A
> Append the backup set to the tape (the default is to replace its current data).

/V
> Verify the backup after writing it.

/R
> Restrict tape access to its owner and *Administrators* and *Backup Operators*.

/D *label*
> Specify a description for the backup set (enclose in quotation marks if there are internal spaces).

/B
> Include the local registry files in the backup.

/HC:ON | OFF
Specifies the hardware compression setting.

/T *type*
Selects the backup type: one of **normal**, **copy**, **incremental**, **differential**, or **daily**.

/L *path*
Specify the log file for this backup operation.

/TAPE:*n*
Use tape drive number *n* (drive numbers may be viewed with the **Properties** button in the **Tape Devices** control panel applet). By default, the system default drive is used.

This is the only option that is valid with **eject**.

path

path [*path*]

Display or set the search path (a semicolon-separated list of directories). The form %**path**% may be used to include the current search path in a modified one.

perms†

perms [*options*] *user files*

Display the specified user's permissions for the specified files.

Options

/S
Recurse subdirectories.

/I
Display permissions corresponding to interactive access.

ping

ping *host* | *IP-address*

Ping the specified system.

pmon†

pmon

Continuously display a list of currently running processes as well as overall system memory and paging statistics.

popd

popd

Return to the directory at the top of the directory stack (and remove it from the stack).

pulist†

pulist [*server*] [*server* ...]

List processes by owner on the specified systems, defaulting to the local system.

pushd

pushd [*path*]

Change the current working directory to the specified directory and save the previous location in a directory stack (return with **popd**). Without an argument, **pushd** displays the current directory stack.

pview†

pview

Display process information in extreme detail (select the process via the resulting window's process pop-up menu).

pviewer†

pviewer

Provide a detailed display of process information (select the desired process from the **Process** list box in the resulting window).

rd

rd [*options*] *path*

Remove a subdirectory. **rmdir** is a synonym for **rd**.

Options

/S

Remove the entire subtree.

/Q

Suppress confirmation prompts.

rdisk

rdisk

Create emergency repair diskette.

regback†

Back up registry hives to disk.

regback *directory*

Back up all registry files to the specified directory (which must *not* already contain registry backup files).

regback *file* **MACHINE** | **USERS** *hive*

Back up the specified hive to the specified file, where *hive* is a subtree of HKEY_LOCAL_MACHINE or HKEY_USERS (as indicated by the preceding keyword).

regrest†

Restore registry hives backed up with the **regback** command.

> **regrest** *backup-dir save-dir*

Replace current registry hives with the information stored in *backup-dir*, saving the current registry files into *save-dir*.

> **regrest** *backup-file save-file* **MACHINE** | **USERS** *hive*

Restore the specified registry hive from *backup-file*, saving the current hive to *save-file*. The system must be rebooted for the new data to become active.

ren

> **ren** *path new-name*

Rename the specified file. **rename** is a synonym for **ren**.

replace

> **replace** *source-files destination* [*options*]

Replace/update files in a destination directory.

Options

/A

Add new files to the destination directory (not valid with /U or /S).

/U

Only update destination files that are older than their corresponding source files.

/S

Recurse subdirectories.

/P

Require confirmation for all replacements.

rkill†

List/manage remote processes. This command requires that the Remote Kill service be running on the remote system.

   rkill /VIEW *host*

List the processes running on the specified remote host.

   rkill /KILL *host pid*

Terminate the specified remote process.

---

route

   route [*options*] [*cmd* [*dest*] [**MASK** *netmask*] [*gateway*]
   [**METRIC** *hops*]]

View or modify the routing table. *cmd* is one of the following:

PRINT
   Display the specified route (or all routes).

ADD
   Add the specified route.

DELETE
   Remove the specified route.

CHANGE
   Modify the specified route.

The netmask defaults to 255.255.255.255, and the metric defaults to 1.

Options

/F
   Clear all gateway entries from the routing table.

/P
   Use with **ADD** to define a persistent route (which survives system reboots).

scanreg†

scanreg /s *search-string item-options* [*options*]

Search the specified registry entities for the specified character string.

Item Selection Options

One or more of these must be specified.

/k

Search key names.

/v

Search value names.

/d

Search value settings (data).

Additional Options

/c

Perform a case-sensitive search.

/e

Require an exact match.

sclist†

sclist [*options*] [*host*]

List services on the specified host (defaults to the local system).

Options

/R

Display running services only.

/S

Display stopped services only.

scopy†

scopy *files destination* [*options*]

Copy files and preserve security settings.

Options

/O

Copy ownership information.

/A

Copy auditing information.

/S

Recurse subdirectories.

showdisk†

showdisk

Display very detailed disk partition information.

showgrps†

showgrps [*domain\\user*]

List the groups of which the specified user is a member.

shutdown†

shutdown *remote-host* | /L [*options*] [*message*]

Shut down a Windows NT system. Include /L to shut down
the local system or specify a remote host as the command's
first argument.

Options

/R

Reboot after shutting down.

/T:*n*

Wait *n* seconds before shutting down (the default is 20).

/Y

Answer yes to all subsequent prompts.

/A

Abort a pending shutdown.

/C

Close open applications without saving data.

---

soon†

soon [*host*] [*seconds*] [**/INTERACTIVE**] *command*

Run a command after a delay period. This command serves as an alternate interface to the Schedule service (see also the **at** command) on the local computer or a remote host.

soon schedules the specified command to run in the indicated number of seconds (see below for defaults). The **/INTERACTIVE** option allows it to interact with the keyboard when executed.

soon /D [*options*]

Set default values for various parameters used by the **soon** command, as indicated by the subsequent options.

Default-Setting Options

/L: *n*

Sets the default delay period for local jobs to *n* seconds (initially 5).

/R: *n*

Sets the default delay period for remote jobs to *n* seconds (initially 15).

/I:ON | OFF

Specifies whether the **/INTERACTIVE** option is the default or not (initially off).

---

sort

> **sort** [*options*] [< *file*]

Sort standard input (use I/O redirection to sort a file).

Options

/R
> Reverse usual sort order (i.e., Z to A, 9 to 0).

/+n
> Start sorting in column *n*.

---

srvcheck†

> **srvcheck** \\ *host*

List all shares and their access permissions on the specified computer system.

---

start

> **start** [*window-title*] [*options*] *command*

Start a command.

Options

/Ddir
> Set the current working directory for the command.

/B
> Start the command as a background process (don't create a new window).

/LOW, /NORMAL, /HIGH, /REALTIME
> Specify the priority class for the new process.

/WAIT
> Start the command and wait for it to complete.

/MIN, /MAX
> Start the command and minimize/maximize the new window (respectively).

/I

Pass the original environment to the command rather than
the current environment.

telnet

telnet *host* | *IP-address*

Initiate an interactive session to a remote host (which must
provide a telnet service).

time

time [*time*]

Set the time to the specified time (prompted if omitted). The
/T option displays the time without modifying it.

timethis†

timethis *command*

Run the specified command and report on its execution
timing data. It is often useful to combine this command with
start /B to time a background command.

tlist†

tlist [/T]

List current processes, in tree format (indicating process
parentage hierarchy) if **/T** is included.

tlist *pid* | *regular-expression*

List module information for the specified process or all
matching processes.

tracert

tracert *host* | *IP-address*

Display the route to the specified destination.

tree

> **tree** *dir* [*options*]

Display the tree structure for the specified directory.

Options

/A

> Use ASCII characters instead of extended graphics characters.

/F

> Include filenames in the display.

type

> **type** *file*

Display file contents.

usrstat†

> **usrstat** *domain*

List domain users and their most recent login times.

ver

> **ver**

Display Windows NT operating system version.

verify

> **verify** [ON | OFF]

Display/set default write verify status.

vol

> **vol** [*x:*]

Display the volume label for drive *x*.

xcopy

> **xcopy** *files destination* [*options*]

Copy directory trees.

Options

/R

> Overwrite read-only files.

/U

> Update mode: only copy files that already exist in the destination directory tree.

/D:*m-d-y*

> Copy only files modified on or after specified date.

/A, /M

> Select files with the archive attribute set, then leave it set or unset (respectively).

/H

> Include hidden and system files.

/S

> Recurse non-empty subdirectories.

/T

> Reproduce the directory tree structure but don't copy any files (excludes empty subdirectories).

/E

> Include empty directories (implies /S unless used with /T).

/V

> Verify the copied data.

/I

> Force the destination to be interpreted as a directory.

/Q, /F

> Produce terse or verbose output (respectively).

/L

List files that would be copied by the command, but don't actually copy any files.

/P

Require confirmation for each destination file.

/K

Reproduce the read-only status of copied files.

/N

Copy using 8.3 (DOS-style) filenames.

/C

Continue copying even if an error occurs.

/Z

Copy network files in a restartable operation.

The Windows NT Scripting Language

Script-Related Constructs

:*label*

> Named location within script (target of **goto** or **call** command).

%*m*

> Argument number *m* (access arguments above the ninth one via the **shift** command).

%~*cm*

> Modified argument *m*, where *c* can be one or more of the following code letters indicating the parts of the argument to use:

f

> Full pathname.

d

> Drive letter only.

p

> Path only.

n

> Filename only.

x

> Extension only.

s

> Use 8.3 (DOS-style) names (valid with **n** and **x**).

$PATH

> Examines the search path in the PATH environment variable and returns the fully qualified pathname for the first match for the argument, returning an empty string if the item is not found.

%*

> Corresponds to all command parameters.

%*var*%
> Value of variable *var* (local or environment).

errorlevel
> Internal variable set by various commands. Often indicates the contents of user input—see the discussion of the **if** command.

Commands Useful in Scripts

call

> **call** *file* | :*label* [*args*]

Run the specified external script file or labeled subroutine within the current script.

choice†

> **choice** [/C:*choices*] [/S] [/T:*c,n*] *prompt-string*

Prompt user to select from a list of choices, using the specified string as the prompt text. Sets the *errorlevel* variable to the selected choice number (starting at 1).

Options

/C:*choices*
> Specify choice letters (the default is **YN**).

/S
> Make choices case-sensitive.

/T:*c,n*
> Select default choice *c* after timeout of *n* seconds.

cls

> **cls**

Clear the screen.

echo

> echo *message*

Display the specified message text on screen. The *message* may not be null. A string consisting solely of a period at right margin is the conventional way to create a "blank" output line.

> echo ON | OFF

Enable or disable command echoing (enabled by default).

exit

> exit

Terminate script immediately (or terminate the current command interpreter if executed interactively).
See also **goto :EOF**.

for

Loop construct.

> for [/D] %%*var* in (*filelist*) do *command*

Loop over a list of files. The specified variable is set to each successive item in the file list each time through the loop.

/D says to match directory names only in *filelist*.

> for /L %%*var* in (*m,j,n*) do *command*

Loop from *m* to *n* by *j*, using the specified variable as the loop index.

goto

> goto *label*

Jump to the named location in the script.

> goto :EOF

Jump to the end of the current script file.

---

if

Conditional command. In all cases, including the **not** keyword inverts the logical expression.

   if [not] **errorlevel** *n command*

Execute *command* if the value of the **errorlevel** variable is/isn't greater than or equal to *n*.

   if [not] **defined** *variable command*

Execute *command* if the specified variable is/isn't defined.

   if [not] **exist** *file command*

Execute *command* if the specified file does/doesn't exist.

   if [not] [/I] *string1 op string2 command*

Execute *command* if the specified string comparison expression is true/false. The available operators are:

==, EQU
  Equal.

NEQ
  Not equal.

LSS
  Less than.

LEQ
  Less than or equal.

GTR
  Greater than.

GEQ
  Greater than or equal.

All comparison operators are case sensitive. **/I** says to perform a case-insensitive comparison.

pause

pause

Pause execution until user presses a key.

prompt

prompt *text*

Set the command prompt to *text*, which can contain the following codes (among others—see **prompt /?**):

$D, $T

Current date, current time.

$G

Greater than sign (>).

$N

Current drive letter.

$P

Current drive and working directory.

$S

Space.

$_

Carriage return.

rem

rem *anything*

Comment line, ignored by the command interpreter.

set

Display/set a variable value.

set [*var*]

Display value of the specified variable (or all defined variables).

set *var=string*

Set the value of a string variable.

set /A *var=numeric-expression*

Set the variable to the result of the evaluated numeric expression.

---

setlocal ... endlocal

setlocal begins a local environment within the script, which is terminated by **endlocal**.

---

shift

shift [*/n*]

Shift script/command arguments down one place, starting at argument *n* (if specified).

The Windows NT GUI

Commands for the GUI
Administrative Tools

Tool	Command
Administrative Wizards	**wizmgr**
Backup Facility	**ntbackup**
Command Prompt	**cmd**
Dfs Administrator	**dfsadmin**
DHCP Manager	**dhcpadmn**
Disk Administrator	**windisk**
DNS Manager	**dnsadmin**
Event Viewer	**eventvwr**
License Manager	**llsmgr**
Network Client Administrator	**ncadmin**
Network Monitor	**netmon**
Performance Monitor	**perfmon**
Registry Editor	**regedt32**
Remote Access Administrator	**rasadmin**
Service Install Wizard†	**srvinstw†**
Server Manager	**srvmgr**
System Policy Editor	**poledit**
Task Manager	**taskmgr**
User Manager	**musrmgr**
User Manager for Domains	**usrmgr**
Windows NT Diagnostics	**winmsd**
WINS Manager	**winsadmn**

Windows NT GUI Tips and Tricks

Using the Mouse

Shift-click (on items)
Select a range of adjacent items.

Control-click (on items)
Select multiple, not necessarily adjacent items.

Shift-click (in window close box)
Close the window and its parents.

Right-click (on item)
Bring up the item's shortcut menu (includes its **Properties**). Pressing Alt-Enter performs the same function for a selected item.

Shift-right click (on an already selected item)
Include the **Open with** selection in the item's shortcut menu.

Alt-double click (on item)
Open the item's **Properties**. Pressing Alt-Enter when the item is selected does the same thing.

Control-double click (on folder)
Reverse the sense of the "Always Open New Folder" browsing option setting.

Shift-double click (on folder)
Open folder in Explorer view instead of the normal browsing view.

Keyboard Shortcuts

Control-Tab, Control-Shift-Tab
Move between the tabs in a multipanel dialog box, in forward and reverse order (respectively).

Backspace (when browsing)
Move up one directory level.

Ctrl-Esc
Bring up the **Start** menu.

F3 (desktop only)
Start the **Find Files or Folders** facility

Shift-Delete (selected items)
Bypass the recycle bin for the currently selected files. You can also make this the default behavior by right clicking on the Recycle Bin and modifying its **Properties**.

Win-R
Open the **Run** dialog box.

Win-F
Open the **Find Files or Folders** facility.

Win-M
Minimize all currently open windows.

Win-Shift-M
Undo a **Win-M** operation.

Win-Break
Open the **System Properties** dialog box.

Win-*x*
Select the desktop items whose names begin with the specified letter in turn (when that key combination is not already defined).

Useful Windows NT Web Sites

Site Lists

- *www.yahoo.com/Computers_and_Internet/Operating_ Systems/Microsoft_Windows/Windows_NT*

- *www.indirect.com/www/ceridgac/ntsite.html*

- *www.netmation.com/listnt.htm*

Windows NT Information

- *www.ntinternals.com*

- *www.ntsecurity.net*

- *www.winntmag.com* (information on available hot fixes plus the latest Windows NT-related news)

- *www.unixnt.com* (integrating Windows NT and UNIX)

- *www.microsoft.com/ntserver* and *www.microsoft.com/ntworkstation*

- *www.microsoft.com/kb* (Microsoft Knowledge Base)

  You may also go directly to the article Q$nmopqr$ via the path *www.microsoft.com/kb/articles/q*nmo/p/qr.*htm* (note that n may be blank).

- *www.windowsnt.digital.com* (Windows NT on Alpha-based systems)

Software Archives

- Aaron's Alpha NT Applications Archive: *dutlbcz.lr.tudelft.nl/alphant/archive.html*

- Beverly Hills Software: *www.bhs.com/download/default.asp*

- The Coast-to-Coast Software Repository: *www.coast.net/SimTel/nt.html*

- Windows NT-Plus: *www.windowsnt-plus.com/shareware*

- WinSite Windows Archive: *www.winsite.com/winnt*

- Nomad Mobile Research Centre: *www.nmrc.org/files/nt* and *snt* (security/hacker-related items)

- Jim Buyens' Windows NT Web Server Tools: *www.primenet.com/~buyensj/ntwebsrv.html* and *sysadmin.html*

- Windows NT Internals Utilities: *www.ntinternals.com/ntutil.htm*

- Service Packs and Hot Fixes: *ftp.microsoft.com/bussys/winnt/winnt-public/fixes* (one subdirectory tree per OS language version)

Index